This is My Name

and I want to write it down before I forget it

ISBN: 978-1-958150-32-0
This is My Name, and I wanted to write it down before I forget it

Published by **Inner Peace Press**
Eau Claire, Wisconsin, USA
www.innerpeacepress.com

This is My Name

and I want to write it down before I forget it

Written by

Barbara Shafer

Illustrations by

Anders C. Shafer

Table of Contents

Prelude: How this book came to be

A year and a half after my father died, my mother was hospitalized. She was suffering from dementia and severe depression, and had stopped eating. I flew from Wisconsin to be with her in Florida, where I stayed for over a week.

Even though she had an Advance Directive, it took four days for my brother and me to convince her doctors not to put a tube in her stomach and to permit her to go home. And, it took another four days to make preliminary home care arrangements, including 24-hour live-in care providers and hospice services. The hospice nurse examined my mother and told me not to expect her to live more than another two weeks. I said my "good-byes" and reluctantly returned to Wisconsin, thinking I would return soon.

Amazingly, my mother lived another two and a half years. Prior to my next visit, I was constantly on the phone with my mother's care provider, talking about her needs, her preferences, and all the day-to-day management issues that arose as she moved into this new phase. When I finally returned to Florida, however, I

Painting by Barbara Shafer

7

learned that there is only so much that one can communicate over the phone.

The day I returned, I walked into the apartment and was taken aback; I almost did not recognize the woman sitting on the sofa. For her entire adult life my mother had worn her hair in the simplest of unadorned styles. The woman in front of me was decked out in the puffiest bouffant "do" possible for the thinning locks of an 84-year-old. Her care provider, who was extremely pleased at having taken her to the beauty salon in advance of my visit, immediately asked me if I liked the way "Lilly" looked. In all those same 84 years, no one had ever called my mother, whose name was Lillian, "Lilly."

The very caring woman who had brought my mother back to life did not have the very basic knowledge of what that life had been: from what Lillian looked like to what she expected to be called.

The care provider did not know that my mother had been a class A golfer and on Sunday afternoons would enjoy nothing more than watching a match on TV. She did not know that my mother, not being on any medication, would have enjoyed a good scotch before dinner, nor did she know, that sweet "Lilly" had been a well-organized "mover and shaker" in her community, the president of every club and organization she ever joined (and there were plenty).

For Lillian to enjoy, as much as possible, her remaining years, the woman in charge of my mother's care should have known all of this and much more. It should have been in writing.

I present to you a book designed for you to fill in a description of "the essential you," or help an essential loved one do that. It is for you, in hopes that, if necessary, in the future, someone will look through it and learn who you are, what is important to you, your beliefs, what you like and what you dislike, and when you want your morning coffee. Have fun with this book, for despite its serious nature the intent is to ultimately keep life "fun."

Before you proceed

This book was put together as a vessel as well as inspiration for its owner. Use it as you will! It was impossible to devise questions for all the information you wish to impart. Please, add any thoughts that come to mind. To that end, each section also offers an extra page for notes.

You should give a trusted family member/friend access information to your: computer, cell phone, tablet. Also give him/her/them your "usernames," "passwords," and answers to computer prompt/security questions.

I did not provide space for your social security and Medicare numbers for safety reasons. This information should also be stored with someone you trust and/or how to access it in hard copy among your possessions and with your will.

I have divided this book into the following sections:

Introductions
My Life
Keeping Me Healthy
Beauty Secrets
Additional Stuff: Services, Professionals, and Institutions
My Eventual Demise

INTRODUCTIONS

This is My Name

I would like to introduce myself, my name is:

My husband_____ wife_____ best friend_____ partner's _____ name is:

He or she calls me:

My friends call me:

I would like it if you called me:
Please do not give me a nickname that I have not chosen.

Here is a picture of me.

Reaching My Next of Kin/Close Friends or Emergency Contacts

Name	Relation	Daytime Phone	Evening Phone	Social Media

This is My Story

To start with... I was born:

Places I lived:

Schools I attended and degrees I received:

Professional/work history:

Memories.... or *I did it my way*
My life's biggest accomplishments and what I like most about myself:

And, what makes me unique?

Life has dealt me a few blows:

Please do what you can to help me stay me!

My Belief System:

My religion_____ is_____ is not_____ important to me.

The synagogue, church, or mosque I attend:

Address:

The clergyman/clergywoman is:

Contact information:

I wish to attend services
Monday @ times:
Tuesday @ times:
Wednesday @ times:
Thursday @ times:
Friday @ times:
Saturday @ times:
Sunday @ times:

Our important holidays are:

The rituals I follow at home:

My Heritage

Specific DNA information can be found at:

My Parent's Names and Information
Mom:

Dad:

My mother's parents
Mother:

Father:

My father's parents
Mother:

Father:

Earlier generations:

My Siblings

Name/partner:
Brag space

daytime phone: *evening phone:*
Email/social media:
Address:

Name/partner:
Brag space

daytime phone: *evening phone:*
Email/social media:
Address:

Name/partner:
Brag space

daytime phone: *evening phone:*
Email/social media:
Address:

Name/partner:
Brag space

daytime phone: *evening phone:*
Email/social media:
Address:

Name/partner:
Brag space

daytime phone: *evening phone:*
Email/social media:
Address:

Let Me Tell You About My Children

Name/partner:
Brag space

daytime phone: *evening phone:*
Email/social media:
Address:

Name/partner:
Brag space

daytime phone: *evening phone:*
Email/social media:
Address:

Name/partner:
Brag space

daytime phone: *evening phone:*
Email/social media:
Address:

Name/partner:
Brag space

daytime phone: *evening phone:*
Email/social media:
Address:

Name/partner:
Brag space

daytime phone: *evening phone:*
Email/social media:
Address:

And Grandchildren

Name/partner:
Brag space

daytime phone: *evening phone:*
Email/social media:
Address:

Name/partner:
Brag space

daytime phone: *evening phone:*
Email/social media:
Address:

Name/partner:
Brag space

daytime phone: *evening phone:*
Email/social media:
Address:

Name/partner:
Brag space

daytime phone: *evening phone:*
Email/social media:
Address:

Name/partner:
Brag space

daytime phone: *evening phone:*
Email/social media:
Address:

Grandchildren (continued)

Name/partner:
Brag space

daytime phone: *evening phone:*
Email/social media:
Address:

Name/partner:
Brag space

daytime phone: *evening phone:*
Email/social media:
Address:

Name/partner:
Brag space

daytime phone: *evening phone:*
Email/social media:
Address:

Name/partner:
Brag space

daytime phone: *evening phone:*
Email/social media:
Address:

Name/partner:
Brag space

daytime phone: *evening phone:*
Email/social media:
Address:

And Great-Grandchildren

Name:
You can brag here, too...
His____ her____   Mom and dad:
Contact information:

Name:
You can brag here, too...
His____ her____   Mom and dad:
Contact information:

Name:
You can brag here, too...
His____ her____   Mom and dad:
Contact information:

Name:
You can brag here, too...
His____ her____   Mom and dad:
Contact information:

Name:
You can brag here, too...
His____ her____   Mom and dad:
Contact information:

Name:
You can brag here, too...
His____ her____   Mom and dad:
Contact information:

Name:
You can brag here, too...
His____ her____   Mom and dad:
Contact information:

Name:
You can brag here, too...
His____ her____   Mom and dad:
Contact information:

And Great Grandchildren (continued)

Name:
You can brag here, too...
His____ her____   Mom and dad:
Contact information:

Name:
You can brag here, too...
His____ her____   Mom and dad:
Contact information:

Name:
You can brag here, too...
His____ her____   Mom and dad:
Contact information:

Name:
You can brag here, too...
His____ her____   Mom and dad:
Contact information:

Name:
You can brag here, too...
His____ her____   Mom and dad:
Contact information:

Name:
You can brag here, too...
His____ her____   Mom and dad:
Contact information:

Name:
You can brag here, too...
His____ her____   Mom and dad:
Contact information:

Name:
You can brag here, too...
His____ her____   Mom and dad:
Contact information:

My Extended Family Matters to Me
(Aunts, Uncles, Cousins)

Name: *Relationship:*   **Partner:**
daytime phone: evening phone:
social media:

Name: *Relationship:*   **Partner:**
daytime phone: evening phone:
social media:

Name: *Relationship:*   **Partner:**
daytime phone: evening phone:
social media:

Name: *Relationship:*   **Partner:**
daytime phone: evening phone:
social media:

Name: *Relationship:*   **Partner:**
daytime phone: evening phone:
social media:

Name: *Relationship:*   **Partner:**
daytime phone: evening phone:
social media:

Name: *Relationship:*   **Partner:**
daytime phone: evening phone:
social media:

Name: *Relationship:*   **Partner:**
daytime phone: evening phone:
social media:

Name: *Relationship:*   **Partner:**
daytime phone: evening phone:
social media:

Name: *Relationship:*   **Partner:**
daytime phone: evening phone:
social media:

The Famous People in My Family Are

The Infamous:

Great Family Stories:

I enjoy looking at photos albums_____. *Would you take some time to join me and let me tell you about the important people in my life, my travels, and* **those wonderful children and grandchildren of mine.**

My Pets

My dog's name is:
Gender:_____ Breed:
I feed him/her_____ times per day.
Food brand and quantity:
I walk him/her _____times per day.
At _____am _____am _____pm _____pm / _____miles
Favorite toys/*likes and dislikes*

My dog's name is:
Gender:_____ Breed:
I feed him/her_____ times per day.
Food brand and quantity:
I walk him/her _____times per day.
At _____am _____am _____pm _____pm / _____miles
Favorite toys/*likes and dislikes*

My cat's name is:
Gender:_____ Type:
I feed him/her_____ times per day.
Food brand and quantity:
Favorite toys/*likes and dislikes*

My cat's name is:
Gender:_____ Type:
I feed him/her_____ times per day.
Food brand and quantity:
Favorite toys/*likes and dislikes*

My bird's name is:
Gender:_____ Type:
I feed my bird:
Special Instructions

Add some pictures here:

My Friends Matter to Me

Name (s):
daytime phone: evening phone:
social media:

Name (s):
daytime phone: evening phone:
social media:

Name (s):
daytime phone: evening phone:
social media:

Name (s):
daytime phone: evening phone:
social media:

Name (s):
daytime phone: evening phone:
social media:

Name (s):
daytime phone: evening phone:
social media:

Name (s):
daytime phone: evening phone:
social media:

Name (s):
daytime phone: evening phone:
social media:

Name (s):
daytime phone: evening phone:
social media:

Name (s):
daytime phone: evening phone:
social media:

My Friends Matter to Me (continued)

Name (s):
daytime phone: evening phone:
social media:

Name (s):
daytime phone: evening phone:
social media:

Name (s):
daytime phone: evening phone:
social media:

Name (s):
daytime phone: evening phone:
social media:

Name (s):
daytime phone: evening phone:
social media:

Name (s):
daytime phone: evening phone:
social media:

Name (s):
daytime phone: evening phone:
social media:

Name (s):
daytime phone: evening phone:
social media:

Name (s):
daytime phone: evening phone:
social media:

Name (s):
daytime phone: evening phone:
social media:

Friends Who Live at a Distance

Name:
Contact information:

Name:
Contact information:

Name:
Contact information:

Name:
Contact information:

Name:
Contact information:

Name:
Contact information:

Name:
Contact information:

Name:
Contact information:

Name:
Contact information:

Name:
Contact information:

Name:
Contact information:

I prefer to stay in touch with family and friends by:
phone_____ text_____ social media_____hand written letters_____

Notes

My Life

Here we go...

I like my mornings to get off to a good start
I like to get up early_____ late_____.
Please do not expect me to wake before:
Or expect me to get out of bed before:
I am a morning person_____ not me_____.
I enjoy a shower_____ bath_____. In the am_____pm_____.
My morning routine includes:

Breakfast I don't eat breakfast_____.
My breakfasts are light_____ the whole nine yards_____.
My favorite breakfasts include:

Actually each day is different____.
But, I need real coffee_____ decaf_____ sugar_____ milk/cream_____
I drink tea_____ real tea_____ decaf_____ sugar_____ milk/cream_____
I drink cocoa_____ other_____
After I eat, I like to:

I get my daily dose of news from a newspaper._____ *Favorite newspaper(s):*

From the TV_____. *Favorite station(s):*

From the radio_____. *Favorite station(s):*

Over the computer_____. Sites:

I have headphones_____ earbuds_____.

And then afternoons
Lunch I eat around:
My lunches are light_____ the whole nine yards_____.
My favorite lunches include:

Including a snack around:
If not otherwise occupied, I might nap in a chair_____ on my bed_____.

When I am in my own space, I enjoy the following activities
I am an avid reader of:
Novels_____ History_____ Mysteries_____ Erotica_____ Biographies_____
Newspapers_____ Poetry_____ Other:

Authors:

Magazines_____
Preferences:

I read books: *in paper volumes_____ on my tablet_____*
on the computer_____

I watch my favorite TV programs: on a streaming service (s)_____

Or watch linear TV_____
My favorite TV Programs are:

Program	Channel	Day (s)	Time
Program	Channel	Day (s)	Time
Program	Channel	Day (s)	Time
Program	Channel	Day (s)	Time
Program	Channel	Day (s)	Time
Program	Channel	Day (s)	Time
Program	Channel	Day (s)	Time
Program	Channel	Day (s)	Time
Program	Channel	Day (s)	Time
Program	Channel	Day (s)	Time
Program	Channel	Day (s)	Time
Program	Channel	Day (s)	Time
Program	Channel	Day (s)	Time

I Mostly Like to Watch:
News____ weather forecasts____ comedies____ dramas____ documentaries_____
game shows ____ soap operas____ reality TV____ talk shows____ true crime _____
popular music shows_____ religious programming_____ reality competition_____
other_____
sports programs_____ including:
Football_____ *Team*:
Basketball_____ *Team*:
Baseball_____ *Team*:
Golf_____ Tennis_____ Bowling_____ Wrestling_____ Other_____

I have no interest in the TV. Please do not just stick me in front of that thing.____

I like listening to the radio_____.
I like to listen with my headphones_____ earbuds_____.
I like talk radio_____music_____news_____other_____.
My favorite stations are:

I stay abreast of the following blogs/podcasts:

My favorite music includes:

I have the following music collections/equipment: CD_____DVD_____
record_____tape_____

My web browser is:

Hands on and Group Activities I Enjoy

I like discussion groups_____ .
Possible topics:

The clubs and affiliations that I wish to remain active in, include:

I would like to join the following clubs or even start one:

I am currently a member at a senior center, or other center:

My volunteer activities:

I currently take classes at:

I draw and paint_____.

I belong to a choir_____.

I am on the following Advisory Board(s):

I would be interested in learning about/or honing my skills at:
Drawing_____ painting_____ scrapbooking_____ knitting_____
woodworking_____ doing genealogical research_____
writing: non-fiction____ memoir____ short stories____ essays____ poetry_____
learning to play or maintaining my skills at an instrument:
keyboard/piano_____ string_____ reed_____
other_____

I am an ardent collector:

I like to play cards_____.
Games:

I play chess____ checkers____ Mahjong____ dominoes____ cell phone games____
other_____ other_____ other_____
other_____
Count me in on that BINGO game_____ absolutely not_____

I enjoy keeping up communication with family and friends:
verbally_____ or with written correspondences_____
Hand written_____ (remember I will need some stationary and stamps)
On my cell phone_____ through texting_____ social media_____
On my computer_____

I practice the following skills:
Include computer skills, arts, crafts, etc.

I practice meditation_____ mindfulness_____ I keep memoir_____
maintain a sketchbook_____ like to photograph my activities_____
other _____

I consider myself a Democrat_____ Republican_____ Independent_____
If I am not under Guardianship, please help me **VOTE.**

My Favorite Forms of Exercise:
My daily exercise regime includes:
Time of day:

When inside
I independently or in a class: use a *stationary bike_____ treadmill_____*
practice yoga_____ Pilates_____ ballet_____ modern dance_____ tai chi_____
swim or exercise in a pool_____weight lift_____ do my physical therapy_____
other_____ other_____ other_____

I belong to a gym_____.

I take classes at:

I play: *pool_____ billiards_____ darts_____ ping pong_____ other_____*

Outside
I like to: *walk_____ jog_____ bike_____ swim_____ other_____*

I participate on teams or in social exercise: *golf_____ tennis_____*
pickle ball_____basketball_____ bocce ball_____ shuffle board_____ other_____

I like to: *fish_____ hunt_____*

The World Outside

Please take me out as often as possible. Yes_____ No thanks_____
I especially like being outside in the summer_____ fall_____ winter_____ spring_____.
I am always cold_____ hot_____.
A blanket around my knees would make me feel warm_____ ridiculous_____.
I enjoy walks_____.
I enjoy car rides_____.
Especially to visit:

I like to garden_____.

Or, go to the park_____.
Favorite:

Or, to the ocean_____.
Favorite beaches:

I love to go out to eat_____.
Favorite restaurants:

I am a born shopper_____.
Favorite stores:

I enjoy going to the movies_____.
Genre:

I enjoy art museums_____ natural history museums_____.
Preferences:

I like the theatre_____. Or, a good concert_____.
Preferences:

Or, the opera_____.
Favorites:

I'd love to see a good sporting event_____.
Preferences:

What I enjoy doing best:

My at home evenings
I enjoy a before dinner drink_____.

And maybe an appetizer_____.
My favorite cheeses are:

Dinners
My favorite foods include:

I have an aversion to the following foods:

I am an evening person_____
Please don't expect me to go to sleep before:_____.
I like to spend my evenings:

Let's Talk Some More About Foods

Foods I am allergic to:

My dietary restrictions include:

I am a vegetarian_____.
I am a vegan_____.
I am kosher_____.
I like my meat rare_____medium_____well done_____.
I like my foods heavily spiced_____.
Please limit my spices_____. In fact none would be best_____.
I use a little_____ no_____ salt.
I should not eat sugar_____.
My foods should be cut up_____chopped_____.
My foods need to be softened_____.
Please follow GERD restrictions_____.
In general, foods I especially like:

And, I do not like:

Snacks I enjoy in the morning:

Snacks I enjoy in the afternoon:

Snacks I enjoy in the evening:

My favorite desserts are:

*I like them all!*_____

I like to sit down to hearty meals_____. Please serve me small portions_____.

Ethnic or cooking styles I particularly like:
Mexican_____ Italian_____ Chinese_____ Greek_____ Japanese_____
French_____ Jewish_____ German (or Slavic)_____ Korean_____ Thai_____
Vietnamese_____ Indian_____ Greek_____ Cuban_____ Mediterranean_____
Other_____ Other_____ Other_____

I drink a supplement to enhance my diet_____.
Brand:

Foods and supplements I eat to maintain a healthy gut:

I like to drink:
_____Cups of coffee, add some sugar____ milk/cream____ time(s) a day:_____
_____am _____am _____am _____pm _____pm _____pm _____pm_____
_____Cups of tea, add some sugar_____ milk/cream_____ time(s) a day:_____
_____am _____am _____am _____pm _____pm _____pm _____pm_____
_____Cups of hot water, time(s) a day:_____
_____am _____am _____am _____pm _____pm _____pm _____pm_____
_____Milk:_____ warm_____ time(s) a day:_____
_____am _____am _____am _____pm _____pm _____pm _____pm_____
_____Glasses of water:_____ with ice:_____ time(s) a day:
_____am _____am _____am _____pm _____pm _____pm _____pm_____
_____Glasses of soda pop:_____ type: _____time(s) a day:_____
_____am _____am _____am _____pm _____pm _____pm _____pm_____
Other:
_____am _____am _____am _____pm _____pm _____pm _____pm_____

I would like an alcoholic drink before dinner_____ after dinner_____.
A beer during a football game would be great, too_____.
Alcoholic preferences including brand:

I like my hard liquor neat_____ on the rocks_____.
Mixed drinks I like:

I smoke cigarettes_____. *brand*:_____ times(s) a day:_____
Cigars_____. *brand*:_____ a pipe:_____ *tobacco brand*:_____
And, in a state where it is legal... I would love some "pot"_____.

Bedding down
My bedding down rituals include:

I keep a diary._____
*I have dentures that need attending to.*_____

And, then sleep
Please leave my door open_____ shut_____.
Please leave my window open in warm weather_____ in cold weather_____
all year round_____.
I like to keep my room at _____ Fahrenheit.
I like air conditioning_____ set at_____.
If possible please do not turn on the air conditioning_____.
Put the fan on high_____ low_____.
I like to sleep with_____ (number of) pillows.
I use a night light_____.
My sleeping habits include:

I usually have to get up____ (number of) times during the night.
I am an insomniac_____.
I have a problem with nighttime incontinence_____.

I like to sleep (position):
Other thoughts

Notes

Keeping Me Healthy

I am allergic to:

I am particularly sensitive to:

Congenital conditions that affect me:

Current prescription medications

Medication
Physician/Clinic: *Phone:*
Pharmacist: *Phone:*
*Dosage:*_____
Time of day: _____am _____am _____pm _____pm

Medication
Physician/Clinic: *Phone:*
Pharmacist: *Phone:*
Dosage:
Time of day: _____am _____am _____pm _____pm

Medication
Physician/Clinic: *Phone:*
Pharmacist: *Phone:*
Dosage:
Time of day: _____am _____am _____pm _____pm

Medication
Physician/Clinic: *Phone:*
Pharmacist: *Phone:*
Dosage:
Time of day: _____am _____am _____pm _____pm

Medication
Physician/Clinic: *Phone:*
Pharmacist: *Phone:*
Dosage:
Time of day: _____am _____am _____pm _____pm

Medication
Physician/Clinic: *Phone:*
Pharmacist: *Phone:*
Dosage:
Time of day: _____am _____am _____pm _____pm

Prescribed medication (continued)

Medication
Physician/Clinic: *Phone:*
Pharmacist: *Phone:*
Dosage:
Time of day: _____am _____am _____noon _____pm _____pm

Medication
Physician/Clinic: *Phone:*
Pharmacist: *Phone:*
Dosage:
Time of day: _____am _____am _____noon _____pm _____pm

Medication
Physician/Clinic: *Phone:*
Pharmacist: *Phone:*
Dosage:
Time of day: _____am _____am _____noon _____pm _____pm

Medication
Physician/Clinic: *Phone:*
Pharmacist: *Phone:*
Dosage:
Time of day: _____am _____am _____noon _____pm _____pm

Medication
Physician/Clinic: *Phone:*
Pharmacist: *Phone:*
Dosage:
Time of day: _____am _____am _____noon _____pm _____pm

Medication
Physician/Clinic: *Phone:*
Pharmacist: *Phone:*
Dosage:
Time of day: _____am _____am _____noon _____pm _____pm

Medication
Physician/Clinic: *Phone:*
Pharmacist: *Phone:*
Dosage:
Time of day: _____am _____am _____noon _____pm _____pm

Prescribed medication (continued)

Medication
Physician/Clinic: *Phone:*
Pharmacist: *Phone:*
Dosage:
Time of day: _____am _____am _____noon _____pm _____pm

Medication
Physician/Clinic: *Phone:*
Pharmacist: *Phone:*
Dosage:
Time of day: _____am _____am _____noon _____pm _____pm

Medication
Physician/Clinic: *Phone:*
Pharmacist: *Phone:*
Dosage:
Time of day: _____am _____am _____noon _____pm _____pm

Medication
Physician/Clinic: *Phone:*
Pharmacist: *Phone:*
Dosage:
Time of day: _____am _____am _____noon _____pm _____pm

Medication
Physician/Clinic: *Phone:*
Pharmacist: *Phone:*
Dosage:
Time of day: _____am _____am _____noon _____pm _____pm

Over the Counter Medication including Vitamins and Supplements

Medication:
Condition:
Dosage:
Time of day: _____am _____am _____noon _____pm _____pm

Medication:
Condition:
Dosage:
Time of day: _____am _____am _____noon _____pm _____pm

Over the Counter Medication including Vitamins and Supplements (continued)

Medication:
Condition:
Dosage:
Time of day: _____am _____am _____noon _____pm _____pm

Medication:
Condition:
Dosage:
Time of day: _____am _____am _____noon _____pm _____pm

Medication:
Condition:
Dosage:
Time of day: _____am _____am _____noon _____pm _____pm

Medication:
Condition:
Dosage:
Time of day: _____am _____am _____noon _____pm _____pm

Medication:
Condition:
Dosage:
Time of day: _____am _____am _____noon _____pm _____pm

Medication:
Condition:
Dosage:
Time of day: _____am _____am _____noon _____pm _____pm

Medication:
Condition:
Dosage:
Time of day: _____am _____am _____noon _____pm _____pm

Medication:
Condition:
Dosage:
Time of day: _____am _____am _____noon _____pm _____pm

Over the Counter Medication including Vitamins and Supplements (continued)

Medication:
Condition:
Dosage:
Time of day: _____am _____am _____noon _____pm _____pm

Medication:
Condition:
Dosage:
Time of day: _____am _____am _____noon _____pm _____pm

Medication:
Condition:
Dosage:
Time of day: _____am _____am _____noon _____pm _____pm

Medication:
Condition:
Dosage:
Time of day: _____am _____am _____noon _____pm _____pm

Medication:
Condition:
Dosage:
Time of day: _____am _____am _____noon _____pm _____pm

Medication:
Condition:
Dosage:
Time of day: _____am _____am _____noon _____pm _____pm

Medication:
Condition:
Dosage:
Time of day: _____am _____am _____noon _____pm _____pm

Medication:
Condition:
Dosage:
Time of day: _____am _____am _____noon _____pm _____pm

Medical Professionals
I have a health care power of attorney:
Contact information:

Internal Medicine / Managing Care Physician:
Clinic:
Phone number:
Address:

Additional Health Manager:
Clinic:
Phone number:
Address:

Dentist:
Clinic:
Phone number:
Address:

Pharmacist:
Clinic:
Phone number:
Address:

Other:
Clinic:
Phone number:
Address:

My clinic portal of health information
Clinic:

These are the Physicians I use
Physician's name and specialty:

Clinic: Phone:
Plan of care:

Physician's name and specialty:

Clinic: Phone:
Plan of care:

Physician's name and specialty:

Clinic: *Phone:*
Plan of care:

Physician's name and specialty:

Clinic: *Phone:*
Plan of care:

Physician's name and specialty:

Clinic: *Phone:*
Plan of care:

Physician's name and specialty:

Clinic: *Phone:*
Plan of care:

Physician's name and specialty:

Clinic: *Phone:*
Plan of care:

I have chronic problems
Problem:
Personal care:

Problem:
Personal care:

Problem:
Personal care:

Problem:
Personal care:

Chronic Conditions (continued)

Problem:
Personal care:

Problem:
Personal care:

Problem:
Personal care:

Problem:
Personal care:

Problem:
Personal care:

Other health services/therapists/specialists/practitioners/insurances

Service and provider:
Clinic:
Phone number:

Service and provider:
Clinic:
Phone number:

Service and provider:
Clinic:
Phone number:

Service and provider:
Clinic:
Phone number:

Service and provider:
Clinic:
Phone number:

Other health services/therapists/specialists/practitioners/insurances (continued)

Service and provider:
Clinic:
Phone number:

Service and provider:
Clinic:
Phone number:

Service and provider:
Clinic:
Phone number:

Service and provider:
Clinic:
Phone number:

Service and provider:
Clinic:
Phone number:

I wear glasses_____

Purchased at: *Phone:*
Prescribing Physician:
Clinic: *Phone:*

I wear dentures_____

Purchased at: *Phone:*
Prescribing Dentist:
Clinic: *Phone:*

I have a hearing aid_____

Left ear:_____ right ear:_____ both ears:_____
Purchased at: *Phone:*
Prescribing Physician:
Clinic: *Phone:*

Transplanted organs
Ongoing care:

Metal Prosthesis
Ongoing care:

My adaptive equipment
Equipment:

Was purchased at: *Phone*
Physician, Clinic: *Phone*

Equipment:

Was purchased at: *Phone*
Physician, Clinic: *Phone*

Equipment:

Was purchased at: *Phone*
Physician, Clinic: *Phone*

Equipment:

Was purchased at: *Phone*
Physician, Clinic: *Phone*

Equipment:

Was purchased at: *Phone*
Physician, Clinic: *Phone*

Equipment:

Was purchased at: *Phone*
Physician, Clinic: *Phone*

Notes

Notes

Beauty Secrets

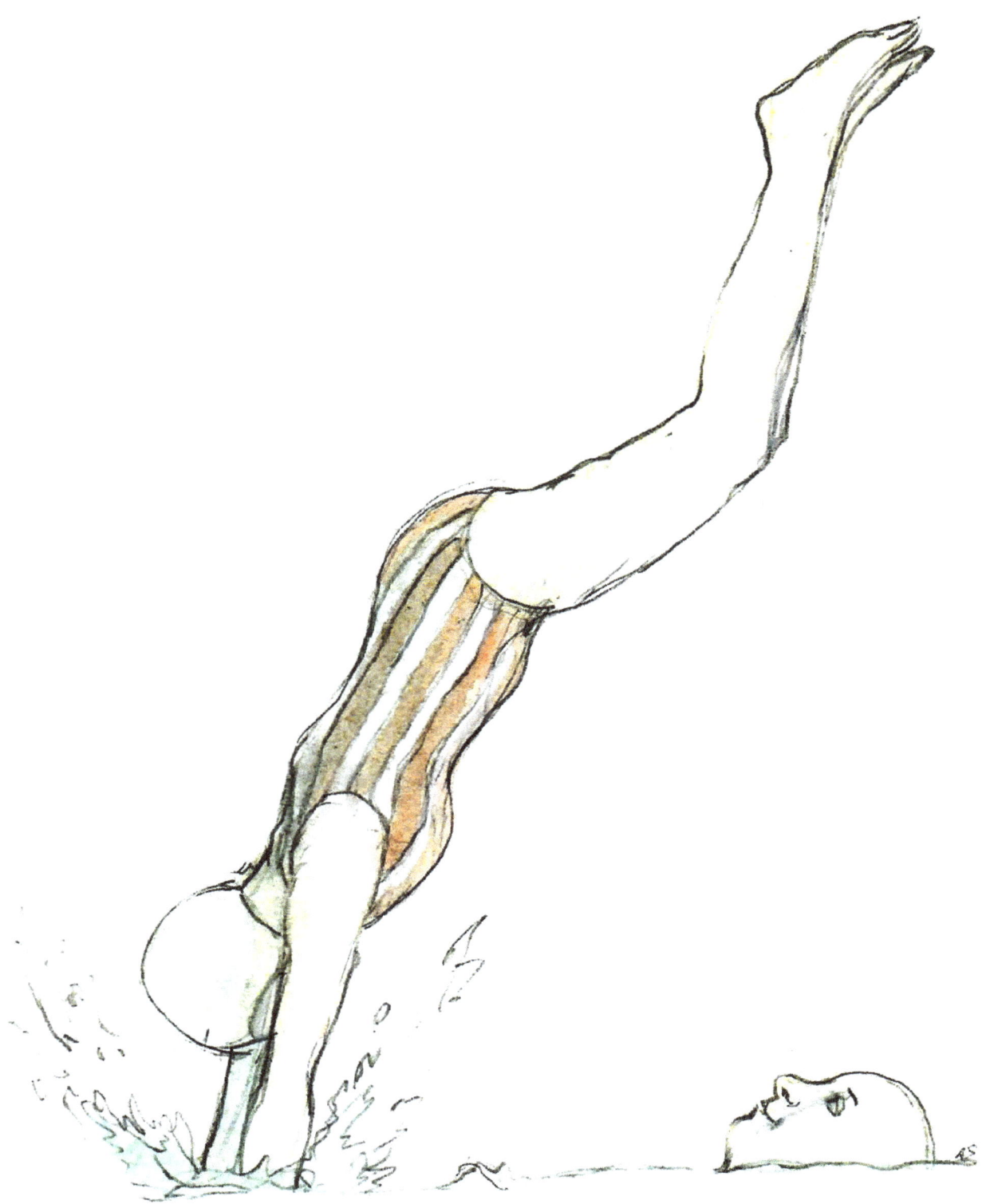

Beauty Secrets
For Women

Hair and Makeup
My favorite beauty salon is:
Beautician: *Phone:*

Address:

I would best describe how I wear my hair as:
Photograph:

I dye it_____. *how often:*
I wear a wig._____
Purchased at:

I usually have my hair done_____. *how often:*

I'd love to have a manicure_____. *how often:*

Pedicure_____. *how often:*

My podiatrist cuts my toe nails_____. *Name:*
Clinic: *Phone:*

I like to wear lipstick_____. *color*:

I like to wear nail polish_____. *color*:

Other make-up I like to use:

My favorite brands
Shampoo:
Face cream:
Body lotion:
Hand cream:
Toothpaste:
Soap:
Bath oil:
Perfume:
Deodorant:
Other:
Other:
Other:
Other:
Other:

My Clothes
Clothes I enjoy wearing every day:

Clothes I enjoy wearing for special occasions:

Clothes I refuse to wear:

When it's cold I like to wear:

When it's hot I like to wear:

I sleep in:

My clothes sizes
Bras:
Undergarments:
Dresses:
Shirts:
Pants:
Shoes:
Jackets and coats:
Gloves/mittens:
Other:
Other:
Other:
Other:
Other:

The right shoes are a must and accessories
Shoes I enjoy wearing every day:

Shoes I enjoy wearing for special occasions:

Shoes I refuse to wear:

I enjoy carrying a hand bag_____.

I like to wear my jewelry_____.

There's lot's more to tell:

Men, Here's Your Turn

Personal Maintenance
My Barbershop is:
Barber: *Phone:*

I like to wear my hair:

I have other hair that needs trimming:

Additional services I appreciate:

I like to have a cut *how often:*

I wear a hair piece____.
Purchased at: *Phone:*

I like to wear a beard_____ mustache_____.
Photograph:

Razor preference
Electric_____ straight edge_____
Purchased at:

Favorite brands
Tooth paste:
Soap:
Shaving cream:
After shave:
Deodorant:
Hair cream:
Cologne:
Razor:
Other:
Other:

Clothes
Clothes I enjoy wearing every day:

Clothes I enjoy wearing for special occasions:

Clothes I wear when no one else will see me:

Clothes I absolutely refuse to wear:

When it's cold I like to wear:

When it's hot I like to wear:

I wear the following type of underwear:

I like to sleep in:

Shoes and accessories
I mostly wear the following shoes:

I wear special dress shoes:

In winter and bad weather I wear:

Shoe brands:

In summer I wear:

I like to wear a tie:

Hats I like:

I carry my money in:

Other items I like to keep on my person:

Additional information:

Clothes sizes

Underwear:	Other:
Undershirts:	Other:
Shirts:	Other:
Slacks:	Other:
Shoes:	Other:
Socks:	Other:
Jackets/coats:	Other:
Gloves:	Other:
Hats:	Other:
Belts:	Other:

Sites or shops I access to find the clothes I like:

Notes

Notes

Additional Stuff
Services, Professionals, and Institutions

Important computer information

I have a PC_____ a hard drive_____ a tablet_____ a cellphone_____.
My phone number is:
Please help me to keep it charged. I access my email through:
My social media handle is:

My network is:

My service provider is:

My web site address is:

My email addresses are:

My favorite browsers are:

My "go to" web sites/program are:

I store my photos:

Online games I enjoy:

The sites I shop at:

I purchased my computer at:
For computer support, I contact:

My important possessions that I always want with me

Photographs:

Paintings:

Dishes:

Furnishings:

Knick-knacks:

Other:

I carry the following credit cards:

    1
    2
    3
    4
    5
    6

I carry the following bank cards:

    1
    2
    3
    4
    5
    6

I carry the following store credit cards:

    1
    2
    3
    4
    5
    6

I Bank at:
contact:
contact:
contact:

My safety deposit box can be found at:
bank name:

My mortgage is with:
contact:

I have outstanding loans with:
contact:
contact:
contact:
contact:

My land line service provider:
my phone number:

My internet service provider:
contact:

My TV service provider:
contact:

My home's energy source:
contact:

Tax consultant:
contact:

Financial advisor:
contact:

Stock broker:
contact:

Attorney:
contact:

Insurance agent:
contact:

My annuities:
contact:
contact:
contact:

My life insurance policies:
contact:
contact:
contact:

My retirement accounts are through:
contact:
contact:

I purchase my health insurance from:
contact:

I purchase my pharmaceutical insurance from:
contact:

My house keeper is:
contact:

My care provider is:
contact:

My lawn care/grounds keeper is provided by:
contact:

My snow removal is provided by:
contact:

My pool is maintained by:
contact:

My furnace is maintained by:
contact:

I contract for the following pest removal services:
contact:

I have belongings stored at:
contact:
contact:

Other:
contact:

Other:
contact:

Other:
contact:

Other:
contact:

Other:
contact:

Other:
contact:

Other:
contact:

Other:
contact:

Other:
contact:

Notes

I have given thought to
My Eventual Demise

My will can be found:

I have the following trusts:

Please place an obituary in the following:

I have made the following financial arrangements:
contact:

contact:

contact:

I prefer a funeral_____ I prefer a memorial service_____.

Perhaps the following people would like to speak:

I have chosen the following funeral home:
Address:

Contact's name:

Church/Synagogue/Mosque:
Address:

Officiant's name:
contact's name if different:

I prefer a relaxed gathering_____.
Address:

Contact's name:

Describe event:

Please play the following music:

Dress me in the following clothes:

I prefer flowers: yes_____ no_____
Please have Memorials sent to:
organization:

organization:

organization:

I prefer cremation: yes_____ no_____
An in-ground burial should be at this cemetery:
address:

Plot Number:

At the cemetery or at the dispersion of ashes
Please have a service_____.
Officiant:

Perhaps the following people would like to speak:

Other thoughts or information I would like to pass on:

Notes